WHAT BIG EARS YOU HAVE!

JIGGS PLAYS WITH HIS CHIMP DOLL.

LET'S TAKE A SPIN IN THE JEEP!

LEAVES ARE FASCINATING.

CHIMP MATH

LEARNING ABOUT TIME FROM A BABY CHIMPANZEE

BY ANN WHITEHEAD NAGDA

AND CINDY BICKEL

Henry Holt and Company

New York

To Marilyn Malin, who always believed in my writing—A. W. N.

To my mom, who taught me compassion, patience, and TLC
Love you—C. B.

Thanks to Lisa Mesple, Roberta Flexer, Candy Hyde, Barb Slenger, and
Susannah Richards for helping with the math.

Henry Holt and Company, LLC
Publishers since 1866
115 West 18th Street
New York, New York 10011
www.henryholt.com

Photo credits: All Denver Zoological Foundation images by Cindy Bickel with the following exceptions—
Ann Rademacher, 2 (bottom), 4; John Edwards, 7, 21, 27 (left), 29, 30 (top left), 31 (top);
M. A. Huffman, 8; Denver Zoo archives, 13, 30 (top right).
We'd also like to thank the following for permission to use photographs from their collections:
Sedgwick County Zoo archives, 9; Lyn Alweis/*Denver Post*, 22.

Distributed in Canada by H. B. Fenn and Company Ltd.

Library of Congress Cataloging-in-Publication Data
Nagda, Ann Whitehead.
Chimp math : learning about time from a baby chimpanzee / by Ann Whitehead Nagda and Cindy Bickel.
1. Time measurement—Juvenile literature. 2. Chimpanzees—Juvenile literature.
[1. Chimpanzees. 2. Animals—Infancy. 3. Time measurement.] I. Bickel, Cindy. II. Title.
QB209.5.N34 2001   529'.7—dc21   00-57529

ISBN 0-8050-6674-8 / First Edition—2002
Printed in the United States of America on acid-free paper. ∞
1 3 5 7 9 10 8 6 4 2

We are grateful for the cooperation of the Denver Zoo, Denver, Colorado.

DRUMMING IS HARD WORK.

I CAN CRAWL!

INTRODUCTION

Chimpanzees are like people in many ways. They use tools and solve problems. They feel happy and sad and angry. In the wild they sleep when they are tired and eat when they are hungry. Chimps have no use for clocks or calendars. But a zoo keeps time records for a baby chimp to make sure he is eating, learning, and growing properly. This book will use time lines, time charts, clocks, and calendars to help tell the story of Jiggs, a chimpanzee that was raised by people at two different zoos. If you want the story without the time records, you can read only the right-hand pages of the book. To learn more about Jiggs hour by hour and day by day, you can look at the left-hand pages as well.

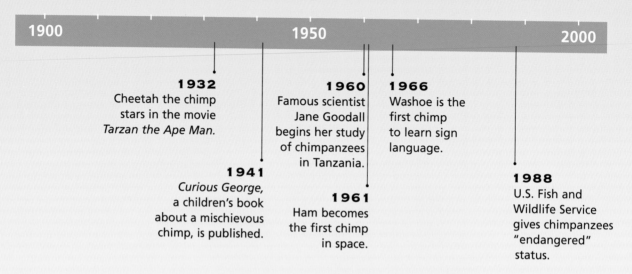

| 1900 | 1950 | 2000 |

1932
Cheetah the chimp
stars in the movie
Tarzan the Ape Man.

1941
Curious George,
a children's book
about a mischievous
chimp, is published.

1960
Famous scientist
Jane Goodall
begins her study
of chimpanzees
in Tanzania.

1961
Ham becomes
the first chimp
in space.

1966
Washoe is the
first chimp
to learn sign
language.

1988
U.S. Fish and
Wildlife Service
gives chimpanzees
"endangered"
status.

A WILD CHIMPANZEE MOTHER
AND HER BABY IN AFRICA.

A time line shows what happened during a certain period of time. The time line above shows things that happened to chimpanzees during the twentieth century. A century is 100 years. When you look at this time line, you can see that Jane Goodall, who is famous for her work with chimps, went to Africa in 1960 to learn about chimpanzees in their own habitat.

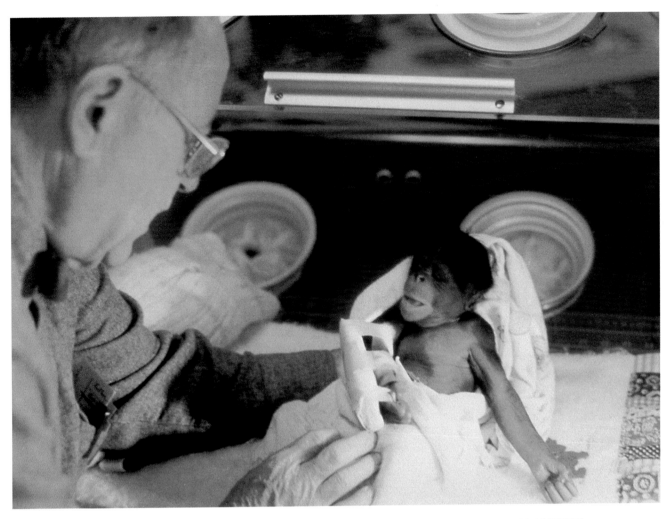

DR. NELSON, A PEDIATRICIAN, EXAMINES THE NEWBORN CHIMPANZEE.

Late one night, a chimpanzee named Holly gave birth to a small, scrawny baby. The staff at the Sedgwick County Zoo in Wichita, Kansas, thought the new baby seemed very weak. They hoped that Holly would pick him up and care for him, but she ignored her baby. Finally, fearing for the tiny chimp's life, they removed him from his mother and placed him in an incubator, which kept him warm and safe.

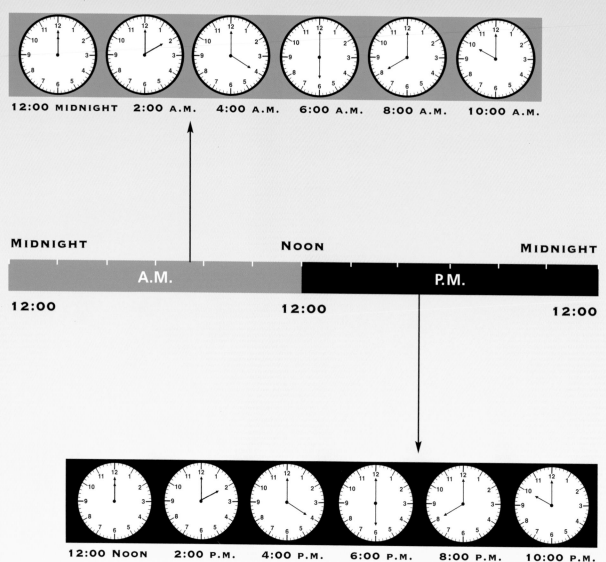

12:00 MIDNIGHT   2:00 A.M.   4:00 A.M.   6:00 A.M.   8:00 A.M.   10:00 A.M.

MIDNIGHT   **NOON**   **MIDNIGHT**

A.M.   **P.M.**

12:00   12:00   12:00

12:00 NOON   2:00 P.M.   4:00 P.M.   6:00 P.M.   8:00 P.M.   10:00 P.M.

The time line on this page is for a much shorter period of time than the one on page 8. This one shows all the times that the baby chimpanzee was fed in one day. A day is 24 hours long.

The chimp was fed every two hours. The first feeding was at midnight. The second feeding was at 2:00 A.M. The letters *A.M.* stand for *ante meridiem,* which means "before noon." The letters *P.M.* stand for *post meridiem,* which means "after noon."

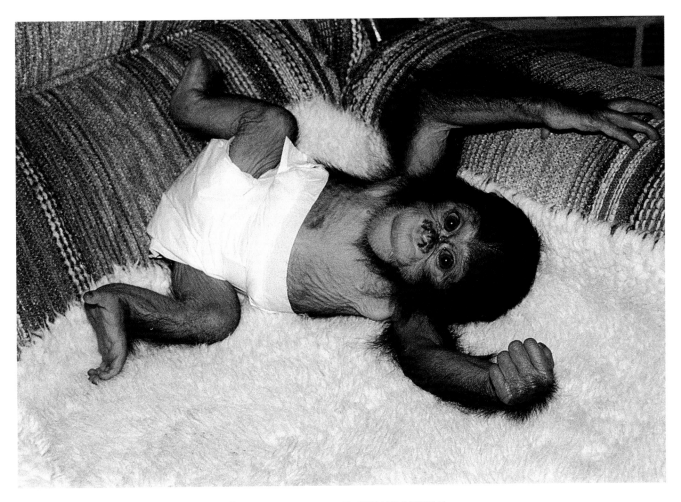

JIGGS, THE BABY CHIMPANZEE.

Dr. R. A. "Jiggs" Nelson, a doctor for human babies, was called in to help care for the fragile baby chimpanzee. The infant was too weak to nurse at first, so Dr. Nelson decided to feed him through a tube. After five days, the baby chimp was stronger and could drink from a bottle. He was fed two ounces of milk every two hours. He was named Jiggs, in honor of the doctor who took such good care of him.

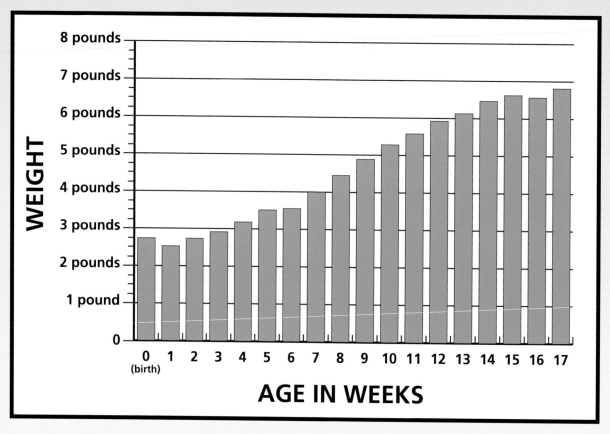

A graph is another way to show what's happened over a period of time. This bar graph shows how the baby chimpanzee's weight changed during the weeks he was at the Sedgwick County Zoo. A week is seven days long. This graph shows what the baby chimp weighed every week.

Jiggs weighed two pounds twelve ounces when he was born, but he lost weight during his first week. The graph shows that he weighed two and a half pounds at one week of age. There are sixteen ounces in one pound, so two and a half pounds is the same as two pounds eight ounces. By the time he was seventeen weeks old, he weighed six pounds thirteen ounces. He had gained four pounds one ounce since birth.

CINDY, A VETERINARY ASSISTANT AT THE DENVER ZOO, FEEDS JIGGS A BOTTLE.

At birth, Jiggs weighed less than he should have. Most newborn chimpanzees weigh around four pounds. Jiggs weighed only two pounds twelve ounces. After a few weeks, he started to gain weight.

Jiggs's mother, Holly, had been loaned to the Sedgwick County Zoo, but both chimps belonged to the Denver Zoo. When Jiggs was seventeen weeks old, he was healthy enough to be moved, so he was driven to Denver, Colorado. Traveling didn't upset the chimp's appetite at all. No matter where he was, he now wanted a bottle every three hours.

FEBRUARY						
SU	MO	TU	WE	TH	FR	SA
						1
2	3	4	5	6	7	8
9	10	11	12	13	14	15
16	17	18	19	20	21	22
23	24	25	26	27	28	

MARCH						
SU	MO	TU	WE	TH	FR	SA
						1
2	3	4	5	6	7	8
9	10	11	12	13	14	15
16	17	18	19	20	21	22
23	24	25	26	27	28	29
30	31					

APRIL						
SU	MO	TU	WE	TH	FR	SA
		1	2	3	4	5
6	7	8	9	10	11	12
13	14	15	16	17	18	19
20	21	22	23	24	25	26
27	28	29	30			

MAY						
SU	MO	TU	WE	TH	FR	SA
				1	2	3
4	5	6	7	8	9	10
11	12	13	14	15	16	17
18	19	20	21	22	23	24
25	26	27	28	29	30	31

JUNE						
SU	MO	TU	WE	TH	FR	SA
1	2	3	4	5	6	7
8	9	10	11	12	13	14
15	16	17	18	19	20	21
22	23	24	25	26	27	28
29	30					

A calendar shows how each month is divided into days and weeks. When Jiggs arrived at the Denver Zoo, he was about four months old. Cindy, who took care of him, wanted to know how old Jiggs was in days rather than in weeks or months, because she kept her records about Jiggs in days. She used a calendar to figure out his exact age.

Cindy had to figure out how many days had passed since Jiggs was born on February 25. Cindy started counting from February 26, when Jiggs was one day old. She stopped counting after she reached June 26, when he arrived at the Denver Zoo. She learned that Jiggs was 121 days old on June 26.

ARE YOU MY MOTHER?

Cindy allowed Kane to help her with Jiggs. Kane was very patient. He let the chimp examine his ears and paws and even take a nap on his back. When Jiggs was teething he wanted to chew on everything—even the dog's ears.

As Jiggs got older, he was able to entertain himself. He could play as long as two and a quarter hours. One morning he started playing at quarter to twelve. He hugged and kissed his chimp doll. He chewed on his colored rings. He climbed on his jungle gym. At two o'clock, Cindy went to get his milk. When she returned with his bottle, Jiggs was fast asleep. He had worn himself out.

DATE	AGE	TIME	REMARKS
Sept. 18	205 days	06:00	Jiggs woke up and chased cat off the bed.
		07:05	He watched TV and ate 2 ounces of banana.
		10:20	Ate cereal, drank 3 ounces of milk. Played with chimp doll.
		12:00	Played on jungle gym, drank 3 ounces of milk, then took a nap.
		15:10	Drank 1 ounce of milk, ate strained carrots.
		17:30	Jiggs ran around house with dog, played game with cat.
		19:40	Drank 5 ounces of milk, then fell asleep for the night.

The chart above records one whole day for Jiggs, from the time he woke up until the time he fell asleep. Cindy often wrote the time in her chart using a 24-hour clock.

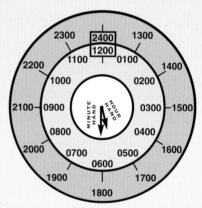

TIME LINE OF A 24-HOUR CLOCK

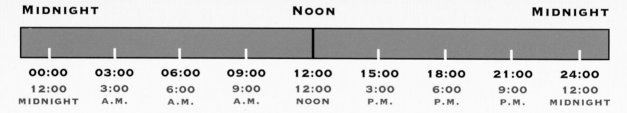

This is a time line of a 24-hour clock. From 1:00 A.M. to 12:00 noon, 24-hour clocks use the same numbers as 12-hour clocks. After 12:00 noon, you can find out the time on a 12-hour clock by subtracting 12:00 from the 24-hour clock's time:

$$17:30 - 12:00 = 5:30$$

so 17:30 is the same as 5:30 P.M.

20

JIGGS LOVES HIS TOYS.

When he was seven months old, Jiggs started to pay even more attention to Cindy's pets. He hugged Kane and ran around the house hanging on to the dog's fur. He played a new game with the cat. Jiggs dangled a piece of fabric over the edge of the bed. The cat swatted at the fabric.

But sometimes Jiggs got in trouble. He chased the cat, then pulled on its ears. He chewed on everything, including electrical cords. He threw his toys. Cindy said "No!" when he chewed on dangerous things. Jiggs stopped and shivered until she touched him and talked to him quietly.

As the days became weeks and the weeks became months, Jiggs grew bigger and stronger and could do more things. On his first birthday, Jiggs was one year old. Here are some other ways of stating his age:

12 months old

52 weeks old

365 days old

8,760 hours old

525,600 minutes old

This is one way to figure out how many hours are in a year:

365 days per year x 24 hours per day = 8,760 hours per year.

This is one way to figure out how many minutes are in a year:

8,760 hours per year x 60 minutes per hour = 525,600 minutes per year.

Most years are 365 days long. Every four years, February has twenty-nine days instead of twenty-eight. These years are 366 days long and are called leap years.

HOW DOES GREEN TASTE?

Cindy wanted to keep Jiggs entertained and out of trouble, so she decided to teach him to paint. But the chimp just stood on the picture and tried to eat the paint. Cindy held his hand and showed him how to use the brush. By the time he was ten months old, he was able to concentrate on a painting for twenty minutes. He could also hold his own bottle of milk and drink from a cup. When Cindy taught him sign language, he learned "food" and "bottle" right away.

On the day Jiggs was one year old, the zoo had a birthday party for him. He was frightened and backed away from the lighted candle on his cake. Cindy gave him some cake, but he spit it out and made a face. Happy birthday anyway, Jiggs!

TIME LINE OF JIGGS'S FIRST YEAR

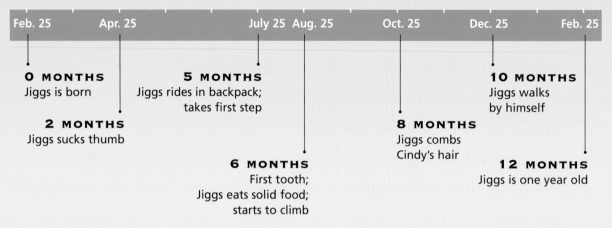

Feb. 25 | Apr. 25 | July 25 | Aug. 25 | Oct. 25 | Dec. 25 | Feb. 25

0 MONTHS
Jiggs is born

2 MONTHS
Jiggs sucks thumb

5 MONTHS
Jiggs rides in backpack;
takes first step

6 MONTHS
First tooth;
Jiggs eats solid food;
starts to climb

8 MONTHS
Jiggs combs
Cindy's hair

10 MONTHS
Jiggs walks
by himself

12 MONTHS
Jiggs is one year old

The time line above shows events that happened in Jiggs's first year. Cindy was curious to see when Jiggs could do things compared to when a wild chimp could do them. She knew when baby chimpanzees in the wild first do certain things, like taking a step or climbing a tree.

Cindy used this information to make a chart like the one below to compare Jiggs's development with that of wild chimpanzees. The chart makes it easy to see that Jiggs did some things "on time" and some things later than a wild chimpanzee.

EVENTS	AGE—WILD CHIMP	AGE—JIGGS
Sucks thumb	2 months	2 months
First tooth	3 months	6 months
Chews and swallows solid food	4 months	6 months
Starts to ride on mother's back	5 months	5 months
Takes first step	5 months	5 months
Climbs up sapling or branch	5 months	6 months
Attempts to comb another's fur	7 months	8 months
Walks alone	9 months	10 months

JIGGS AND HIS FRIEND GIORGIO PLOT MISCHIEF.

When Jiggs was fourteen months old, a jaguar cub named Giorgio joined him in the nursery. Cindy took both babies home with her at night. When Giorgio cried, Jiggs held the cub in his arms to comfort him. Jiggs helped hold the bottle when Cindy fed the little jaguar.

Giorgio and Jiggs loved to chase each other. Jiggs liked to hit the washing machine as he ran by because of the loud *boom* it made. The jaguar watched when Jiggs climbed the floor lamp and slid back down. When Giorgio tried to chew on the electrical cord, Jiggs took it away. He knew that wasn't allowed.

Jiggs was very protective of his jaguar cub. If a person Jiggs didn't know well tried to pick up Giorgio, Jiggs would swing his arms, bare his teeth, hoot, and charge. If a little smack didn't make the person back off, Jiggs would bite.

Feb.	Mar.	Apr.	May	June	July	Aug.	Sep.	Oct.	Nov.	Dec.	Jan.	Feb.	Mar.	Apr.	May

0 MONTHS
Jiggs is born
Feb. 25

6 MONTHS
Climbs ladder of
jungle gym;
climbs out of crib

10 MONTHS
Paints pictures;
learns sign
language

14 MONTHS
Feeds jaguar bottle;
mops floor;
brushes teeth;
climbs pole lamp

7 MONTHS
Watches TV;
looks at books

During the time Jiggs spent at the Denver Zoo, he learned many skills that a chimp in the wild wouldn't learn. This time line shows some of them. At seven months, he could watch TV and look at books. At fourteen months, he fed the baby jaguar a bottle just like Cindy did. Of course, climbing a pole lamp wasn't something he learned by watching Cindy. He figured that out on his own after he learned how to climb trees and exercise on his jungle gym.

JUST HANGING AROUND.

JIGGS GIVES GIORGIO
A BOTTLE.

JIGGS BRUSHES HIS TEETH.

HE MOPS THE FLOOR.

Jiggs always watched everything that Cindy did and tried to copy her. When she brushed her teeth, he wanted to brush his teeth. He helped her fold laundry. He cleaned the nursery floor with a wet mop. Of course, he tried to drink the water in the bucket first!

To get him ready to move from the nursery to the primate house with the zoo's other apes and monkeys, Cindy had to teach Jiggs to eat monkey biscuits. She tried soaking them in apple juice. He sucked the juice out and threw away the biscuits. She coated them with yogurt, but he still wouldn't eat them. Finally Cindy ate a biscuit, and Jiggs ate one too.

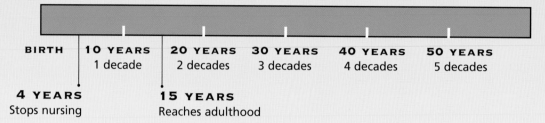

BIRTH	10 YEARS	20 YEARS	30 YEARS	40 YEARS	50 YEARS
	1 decade	2 decades	3 decades	4 decades	5 decades

4 YEARS
Stops nursing

15 YEARS
Reaches adulthood

Time passes and a baby chimpanzee grows up. A baby jaguar grows up too, but on a different time schedule. A chimpanzee doesn't become an adult until he is fifteen years old, while a jaguar takes only four years.

In the wild, a chimpanzee usually lives for three to four decades, or 30 to 40 years. A decade is ten years. A chimp living in a zoo, however, may live for more than five decades. So a chimp in a zoo can live quite a bit longer than one in the wild. The amount of time that Jiggs spent in Wichita and in Denver was just a small part of his whole life.

TIME LINE OF A JAGUAR'S LIFE IN DECADES

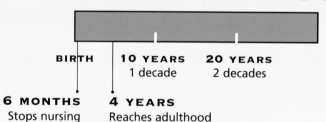

BIRTH	10 YEARS	20 YEARS
	1 decade	2 decades

6 MONTHS
Stops nursing

4 YEARS
Reaches adulthood

A jaguar like Giorgio, Jiggs's friend, can live for up to 22 years in a zoo. This is a little more than two decades. In the wild, a jaguar may live for six to nine years, or less than one decade. Giorgio left the zoo nursery when he was six months old and stayed in the feline (wildcat) exhibit at the Denver Zoo until he was two years old. Then he moved to a zoo in Seattle.

GIORGIO CLIMBS A TREE WHEN HE'S SIX MONTHS OLD.

When Jiggs was sixteen months old, he moved to the primate house. Cindy stayed with him during his first day there. When she left, he screamed. The next day, he clung to her when she came to visit. After several days, a house cat named Zipper was put in with him. The cat slept next to Jiggs, and they played together in the hay. Sometimes Jiggs hugged the cat and wouldn't let him get away, but the chimp had stopped screaming.

After a month at the primate house, Jiggs was taken to the Cheyenne Mountain Zoo in Colorado Springs to join their troop of chimps. In the wild, chimpanzees stay with their mothers for about seven years. Jiggs still needed a mother. Cindy missed Jiggs, but she knew it was best for him to be with other chimpanzees. He was adopted by an older female who took good care of him.

SURPRISE!

CINDY PLAYS WITH JIGGS IN
THE PRIMATE EXHIBIT.

JIGGS PLAYS WITH
HIS PAL GIORGIO.